George Rose

The Trial of George Rose

George Rose

The Trial of George Rose

ISBN/EAN: 9783744689670

Printed in Europe, USA, Canada, Australia, Japan

Cover: Foto ©Suzi / pixelio.de

More available books at **www.hansebooks.com**

THE

TRIAL

OF

GEORGE ROSE, Esq.

SECRETARY TO THE TREASURY, &c.

FOR EMPLOYING

MR. SMITH,

A PUBLICAN IN WESTMINSTER,

UPON A LATE

WESTMINSTER ELECTION,

AND NOT PAYING HIM;

On which he was, on Thurfday the 21ft of July, 1791,

Caſt in the Court of

KING's BENCH,

BY A SPECIAL JURY,

In the Sum of One Hundred and Ten Pounds Five Shillings!

TAKEN IN SHORT HAND,

By A BARRISTER.

☞ This is the moſt curious TRIAL ever yet publiſhed, for diſplaying the ARTS of our HEAVEN-BORN MINISTER, to obtain his CANDIDATES SEATS in PARLIAMENT.

LONDON:

PRINTED FOR J. RIDGWAY, YORK-STREET, ST. JAMES'S
SQUARE.

1791.

LORD JOHN RUSSELL.

My Lord,

THE following Trial is peculiarly interefting to you. The Hampfhire Treafury Opponent of the illuftrious Houfe of
Ruffel, by ftanding Trial with a fimple
Publican, has not only blackened his Character for ever, as an upright Statefman,
but he has confiderably foiled the ermine
of Mr. Pitt's purity, in allowing it to
be proved in a Court of Juftice, where
the King, his mafter, is, in the eye of the
law, omniprefent, that his *virtuous, immaculate,* and *heaven-born Minifter,* was
privy to tranfactions, which, if we may
believe the following words of the great
Locke,

Locke, is a *high breach of trust*, and
therefore he ought no longer to be trusted!

    " He (the perfon vefted with the exe-
" cutive power, *i. e.* the *Premier)* acts
" contrary to his truft, when he either
" employs the force, treafure, and offices
" of the Society, to corrupt the Repre-
" fentatives, and gain them to his pur-
" pofes; or *openly pre-engages the Electors,*
" and *prefcribes to their choice,* fuch whom
" he has, by *folicitations, threats, promifes,*
" or *otherwife, won* to his *defigns,* and *em-*
" *ploys them* to *bring in fuch who have pro-*
" *mifed, before-hand, what to vote,* and
" *what to enact.*

    " Thus, to *regulate Candidates* and *Elec-*
" *tors,* and new model the way of Election,
" what is it but to cut up the Govern-
" ment by the roots, and poifon the
                  " very

" very fountain of public fecurity ? For
" the people having referved to themfelves
" the choice of their Reprefentatives, as
" a fence of their properties, could do it
" for no other end, but that they might
" always be freely chofen, and fo chofen,
" freely act and advife, as the neceffity of
" the Commonwealth, and the Public
" Good fhould, upon examination and
" mature debate, be judged to require.
" This, thofe who give their votes before
" they hear the debate, and have weighed
" the reafons on all fides, are not capable
" of doing.

" To prepare fuch an Affembly as this,
" and endeavour to fet up the *declared*
" *abettors of his own will*, for the true Re-
" prefentatives of the People, and the
" law-makers of the Society, is certainly
" as great a breach of truft, and as per-
" fect

" fect a defign to fubvert the Government,
" as it is poffible to be met with. To
" which, if one fhall add, *rewards* and
" *punifhments*, vifibly employed to the
" *fame end*, and all the *arts* of *perverted*
" *law* made ufe of, to *take off* and *destroy*
" all that ftand in the way of fuch a de-
" fign, and will not comply and confent
" to betray the liberties of their country,
" it will be paft doubt what is doing.

" What power they ought to have in
" the Society who thus employ it, con-
" trary to the truft went along with it,
" in its firft inftitution, is eafy to deter-
" mine; and one cannot but fee, *that he,*
" *who has once attempted any fuch thing as*
" *this, cannot any longer be trufted.*"

LOCKE's *Treatife on* CIVIL GOVERNMENT.

In perufing this curious Trial, my Lord,
                                          you

you will perceive some facts *wonderful,* some *ludicrous,* some very alarming to the *liberties* of the *People,* and *highly injurious to* HIS MAJESTY's *Exchequer!* Your Lordship will read, with the utmost risible indignation, of a *Treasury Secretary* employing a *Publican* for *Election purposes,* in the presence not only of his *brother Secretary,* but in that of his master, the *Prime Minister of the British Empire!* Your indignant risibility, my Lord, will be greatly heightened, when you read of a *Treasury Messenger, suggesting, advising,* and *dictating* to the *all-wise* and *haughty Minister* himself, and his two *sapient Secretaries!* Your Lordship will be shocked for the *Freedom* of *Election,* when you read of many *other* persons besides Smith, *being employed by the Treasury,* in that Election ; Mr. Frost declaring in Court, " that he kept a *distinct* account of " *those persons* which the Treasury employed

B   from

" from thofe which he, as Lord Hood's
" Agent, employed!"

But how, my Lord, muſt you be alarm-
ed, when you read of a *Treaſury Secretary*,
Mr. Roſe, declaring to *Mr. Froſt*,

" *That there was ſomething of a PROSECU-*
" *TION going on with the EXCISE againſt*
" SMITH, *(the* PLAINTIFF *in this Aꝰion) and as*
" *a mark of truſt and confidence THEY had in*
" *him, THEY HAD INTERFERED, and*
" *STEPT IN TO SERVE HIM.*"

Can your Lordſhip peruſe this without a
pauſe, at the groſs enormity, at the high a-
trocity of ſuch a meaſure ? At a crime of the
utmoſt magnitude, of the deepeſt dye, againſt
the *Public Revenue*, to ſerve the corrupt pur-
poſes of Eleꝰioneering intrigue ? No, my
Lord; you and every other good Citizen muſt
exclaim, " No wonder that the People are
oppreſſed

oppreffed with additional burdens, owing, not more to ufelelefs armaments, which ferve but to degrade us; to ufelefs places, which ferve but to corrupt us; than to a defective Revenue, which ferves but to enflave us---a Revenue often rendered defective by the *partiality* of its collection; by our *virtuous* Miniftry *remitting* the *Fines* of *Excife* to thofe who drudge in their venal fervice; whilft, no doubt, all its terrific and grinding fangs are fpread over thofe who are too independent to be their tools, and are crufhed in pieces, by *Excife*, from their obftinate virtue!"

There is not, my Lord, an honeft man in the whole Empire, that will not applaud you, or your friends, in bringing forward this bufinefs, by *parliamentary investigation.* The Excise, in its mildeft mode of collection, fhews much of the

barbarity

barbarity of the *burglar*; but, when cherifhed, ftrengthened, let loofe, and led on by a vindictive Adminiftration, againft their Opponents, it fetters and dungeons its victims with the cruelty of a tyrant; it ftabs with the dark malice of the affaffin; and devours with the ferocity of the tyger!

The only argument which Mr. Rofe's friends can advance to exculpate him on Smith's Excife-fine, is fimilar to what Mr. Erfkine faid in alleviation of his conduct, of at all interfering in the Weft-minfter Election.

The accomplifhed Counfel generoufly urged in the Secretary's defence, although againft him, that he might have engaged in this Election-bufinefs from the pureft motives, in endeavouring to trace out, and

and detect the various iniquities commit-
ted ; fo that a Bill, then in agitation, for
the improvement of Elections in Weftminfter, might be much amended, by the
Secretary's deep knowledge of all the
illegal and corrupt proceedings !

In like manner, my Lord, Mr. Rofe might
have wifhed to ferve the State as well as his
quondam friend, Smith, refpecting the *Excife
fine*; that by *once* pardoning a fellow fubject from the unmerciful rigours of that
odious law, and *viewing his raptures*, it
would act as a grand fympathetic ftimula-
tive, *to remit all Excife fines whatever*; be-
fides, perhaps, *reforming* the *whole of that
Britifh inquifitorial code*, and *quoting Smith's
former oppreffion*, and *prefent happinefs*, in
Parliament, *in fupport* of the policy and
neceffity of that very *reform !*

But, my Lord, however that may be, I
wifh

wifh you and your friends to *profecute*
with *impartial zeal*, this *iniquitous* and *very*
flagrant bufinefs. The *alledged* enormities
of Haftings, however vile and multifa-
rious they really might be proved, *are*
nothing to that charge against Mr. Rofe.

Simplified, my Lord, I underftand the
Excife affair between Mr. ROSE and Mr.
Smith, was this—

Mr. Smith was under the *lafh* of the
Excife, in a fine of *Fifty Pounds*, for *brew-*
ing fome Ale for *his family*, which it feems
no *Publican, Taverner*, or *Innbolder*, has
a right, on *any pretext*, to do.

My Lord, on that *ftrange* tranfaction
I fhall make no more remarks than this:

That after near *three years* of EXCISE
JUDGMENT

JUDGMENT being *pronounced*, Mr. Smith has *only* paid *Twenty-five Pounds* into the Exchequer, of the *Fifty Pounds* awarded by that Board againſt him."

What is the reaſon of this *partiality*, or ſpeaking in the mildeſt manner, of this *ſhameful* LAXITY ?

For the ſake of your country, for the ſake of your illuſtrious family, and your worthy ſelf, inſtitute a *Parliamentary Enquiry* into this vile buſineſs. There is evidence ſufficient to prove it, in the moſt heinous point of view.

MY LORD,

I am, with Reſpect

and Admiration of

Your Character and

Conduct,

YOUR LORDSHIP'S

Moſt obedient Servant,

July 28, 1791.　　　THE EDITOR.

LORD KENYON, AND A SPECIAL JURY.

COUNSEL FOR THE PLAINTIFF,

Meffrs. ERSKINE, MINGAY, and BALDWIN.

COUNSEL FOR THE DEFENDANT,

Meffrs. BEARCROFT and WOOD.

ATTORNEY FOR THE PLAINTIFF,

Mr. GROVE, *Villers-ftreet, Strand.*

ATTORNIES FOR DEFENDANT.

Meffrs. CHAMBERLAYNE and WHITE, Solicitors to the Treafury.

NAMES OF THE SPECIAL JURORS.

1. JOHN STEPHENSON, of *Lower Charles-ftreet,* Efq.
2. NATHANIEL CONANT, of *Lamb's Conduit-ftreet,* Efq.
3. JOSEPH BALLARD, of *Bedford-Row,* Efq.
4. SAMUEL HAWES, of *Major Fourbes's Paffage,* Shoe-Maker.
5. HENRY DIXON, of *Silver-ftreet,* Broker.
6. WILLIAM DAWBNEY, of *Carnaby-ftreet,* Grocer.
7. HENRY FERNELL, of the fame place, Tallow-chandler.
8. RICHARD HEATH, of *Berwick-ftreet,* Coach-maker.
9. WILLIAM LONGSDALE, of *Broad-ftreet,* Cabinet-maker.
10. WILLIAM JEFFERY, of the fame place, Mercer.
11. THOMAS HANKIN, of *Leicefter-fields,* Gent.
12. ANTHONY GERNER, of *Oxford-ftreet,* Glafs-man.

TRIAL

OF

GEORGE ROSE, Esq.

AT THE SUIT OF

MR. SMITH,

A PUBLICAN IN WESTMINSTER,

For Bufinefs done in the late Contefted Election for Weftminfter, Feeding Lord Hood's Friends, &c.

SMITH againft ROSE.

MR. BALDWIN, on the part of the Plaintiff, opened the pleadings. The Declaration ftated, that the Defendant, on the
19th of April, 1791, at Weftminfter,
was indebted to the Plaintiff in the fum
of *One Hundred and Ten Pounds, Five
Shillings*, of lawful money of Great Britain, for the work and labour, care, diligence, and attendance of the Plaintiff,

C   before

before that time done, performed, and beftowed, by him the faid Plaintiff, in and about the bufinefs of the faid Defendant, for the Defendant, and at his fpecial inftance and requeft.

And being fo indebted, he, the faid GEORGE ROSE, in confideration thereof, afterwards, to wit, on the fame day and year aforefaid, undertook and faithfully promifed the Plaintiff to pay him the faid fum of One Hundred and Ten Pounds, Five Shillings, whenever he, the Defendant, fhould be thereunto afterwards requefted.

There were other Counts in the Declaration, upon the *Quantum Meruit*—alfo for money paid, laid out, and expended—for money had, lent, and advanced—and on the balance of Accounts between the parties.

To this Declaration, the Defendant pleaded

pleaded, that he made no such promise, and thereupon issue was joined.

Mr. ERSKINE opened the Case as follows:

May it please your Lordship, and you, Gentlemen of the Jury,

I am a Counsel for the Plaintiff, Mr. GEORGE SMITH, who is a Publican of character and reputation, in King-street, Westminster, where he has resided near twenty-seven years, and he has been sixteen years Master of the *Star and Garter* public house. He is Master also of the livery-stables adjoining.

The Defendant, Mr. GEORGE ROSE, is a *Member of Parliament, one of the Joint Secretaries to the Treasury, Whitehall*, and lives in Palace-yard, Westminster.

Gentlemen, this Action is brought, in order to recover the sum of 110l. 5s. for the work and labour, diligence and attention of the Plaintiff, from the 21*st of September*, 1789, to the 17*th of April*, follow-

C 2 ing;

ing; which, you will find, makes up the
fpace of *Thirty Weeks*, at *Ten Shillings and
Sixpence per day*, in difcovering and collecting proofs of a multitude of bad votes
that were polled for Lord JOHN TOWN-
SHEND, at a late contefted Election for the
City of Weftminfter. The Plaintiff performed this work at the fpecial inftance
and requeft, and under the particular direction of the Honourable Gentleman who
is the Defendant in this caufe.

When I tell you that Mr. ROSE is one
of the *Secretaries to the Treafury*, and that
this Action is brought to recover, on his
Retainer, a fum of money; *a great number
of* OBSERVATIONS might prefent themfelves to a mind difpofed to *mifchief* or to
malice; or to *fcatter infinuations in a* PUB-
LIC PLACE. I will not do fo; becaufe the
queftion you have to try will be this---
" Whether Mr. GEORGE ROSE, of the
Treafury," *no matter from what motives,*
" employed the Plaintiff?" He might have
engaged

engaged Mr. Smith in this bufinefs, from
very juftifiable motives.

.For inftance—from *private friendfhip*;
or, as about that time a Bill was about
to be brought into Parliament, for the
purpofe of making fome *alteration* in the
.Mode of *electing Members of Parliament* to
reprefent the City of Weftminfter, Mr.
Rose, from the moft honourable motives,
might have employed the Plaintiff to detect bad votes, *with a view to gain in-
formation on the fubject, by way of* Foun-
dation *for the* Bill.

Gentlemen, I would much rather that
you fhould impute the conduct of the
Defendant, in this bufinefs, to a *proper*
than to an *improper* motive. If the Defendant is fuppofed to have *bufied* himfelf
in that Election, becaufe my Lord Hood
was looked on to be more the friend of
Government than his Noble and fuccefs-
ful Opponent; and if this Retainer
was to be paid *out of the* PUBLIC
PURSE,

PURSE, it would *not be very honourable for* Mr. Rose; and therefore I do not make any fuch charge.

Gentlemen, it is enough for me that the Plaintiff was retained, and that his houfe, the *Star and Garter*, was opened by the *directions* of Mr. Rose. In 1788, it is well known to us all, there was a ftrong con-tefted Election for a Member to reprefent the City of Weftminfter in Parliament. The Candidates, on the occafion, were, Lord JOHN TOWNSHEND and Lord HOOD. As I have juft obferved, the Plain-tiff's houfe, the *Star and Garter*, was open-ed for the accommodation of Lord HOOD and his Friends, at that Election: and, as I have alfo obferved, this was *done* at the *particular requeft* of Mr. ROSE. In con-fequence of this order, a confiderable ex-pence was incurred, for *good Eating and Drinking*. The Plaintiff made out his Bill on that account, and *that* Bill was very honourably paid. The Plaintiff now ap-plies for the amount of *another Bill*, for

other

other services performed at the *request* of Mr. ROSE, subsequent to that Election.

Gentlemen, although I see Mr. WHITE (*the Solicitor to the Tresaury*) sitting before me, I infer *nothing from that circumstance*, for who would not, on any occasion, be glad to employ so able an Attorney.

[This excited some mirth; and Mr. *White* acknowledged his approbation of the complement, in a profound bow to Mr. *Erskine.*]

Gentlemen of the Jury, all that I have to observe to you is, that Mr. GEORGE ROSE has made a *promise* which he has *not yet performed*, and which it is the object of this action to *compel him to perform.* I impute nothing to those who defend this action, because they are very *honourable* Men. I impute nothing whatever to Mr. GEORGE ROSE, except that he has not paid my Client what he *ought* to have paid him; and which I hope you, Gentlemen of the Jury, will *compel* him to pay. I shall call my Witnesses, and if they can be shaken

in

in their characters, or in their evidence, that will be matter of obfervation for my Learned Friend.

Gentlemen, I fhall only make one other obfervation, which is, that I am not a little furprized that no Money has been paid into Court. Nothing remains but that I fhould call my Witnefses and prove my Cafe ; which will entitle me to your Verdict.

EVIDENCE for the PLAINTIFF.

GEORGE CLUBB was called by Mr. MINGAY ; but not immediately appearing, Mr. ERSKINE obferved that he was, no doubt, a "*knocking-down* fellow," one of the Meffengers to the Treafury ; and therefore a Man whom the *Treafury* might fafely intruft with *any Bufinefs.*

[The Evidence of this *difinterefted* Gentleman was fo *interefting*, and made fo ftrong an Impreffion on every one who heard it, that it may not be improper to give it in detail, togetherwith the queftions that were put to him.]

EXAMINED

EXAMINED by Mr. *MINGAY.*

Q. Is your Name George Clubb, Sir ?

A. It is.

Q What are you, Clubb ?

A. A Meſſenger to his Majeſty's Treaſury.

Q. Do you recollect the conteſted Election between my Lord Hood and Lord John Townshend ?

A. Perfectly, Sir.

Q. Do you know George Smith, the Maſter of the *Star and Garter, in King Street, Weſtminſter,* the Plaintiff in this Action ?

A. Very well, Sir.

Q. Was his houſe open for my Lord Hood and his Friends at that Election ?

A. I was a friend to my Lord Hood and *alſo a friend* to Mr. Smith.

Q. Is that an anſwer to my queſtion, Sir ? I aſk you, Sir, upon your Oath, whether Mr. Smith's houſe was not open for my Lord Hood and his Friends during that conteſted Election between him and Lord John Townshend ?

A. His houſe was opened.

Q. By whoſe order ?

A. By the order of that Gentleman,

D   *(pointing*

(pointing at Mr. Froſt the Solicitor) I went
to Mr. Smith, and told him as a friend,
" Open your houſe immediately---I will be
reſponſible for a *Buttock of Beef, a Ham,
and a Fillet of Veal*."—

(This excited a burſt of Laughter.)

Q. Do you know Mr. Rose?

A. I *know* Mr. Rose *perfeƈtly well*; he
is one of the *Secretaries of the Treaſury*.

Q. Did you ever ſee him at Mr.
Smith's?

A. I never did.

Q. Did Mr. Rose *order* you to go to
Mr. Smith, and tell him to open his houſe
for my Lord Hood?

A. He was *angry* for *my mentioning* that
Mr. Smith's houſe was to be opened.

Q. Why did you deſire Mr. Smith to
open his houſe?

A. I wiſhed to do Mr. Smith good.

Q. *Did you ever carry any meſſage from*
Mr. Smith to Mr. Rose?

A. I did.

Q. What did Mr. Rose ſay?

A. He.

A. He said he was troubled with this man's nonsense ; and I once saw him take one of Mr. SMITH's *Letters and throw it into the fire.*

Q. Do you know that the Plaintiff's Bill was delivered to Mr. ROSE ?

A. I do not remember the Plaintiff's Bill being delivered to Mr. ROSE. Mr. SMITH has been paid his two Bills.

Q. By whom ?

A. Mr. FROST the Solicitor paid him the one, and Mr. JACKSON the other.

Q. Do you know from WHAT SOURCE *this money came ?*

A. It was raised by a SUBSCRIPTION *of* GENTLEMEN.

Q. Of *what* GENTLEMEN ?

A. Of those Gentlemen who chose to subscribe to it.

Q. Were *you* a Subscriber ?

A. I was not.

Q. Was Mr. ROSE a Subscriber ?

A. I don't know that he was.

Q. What occasion was there for a *Sub-scription ?*

A. Mr. *Frost's* Order was refused by Mr. SMITH. He would not take Mr. FROST's

Note,

Note, becaufe it was not fufficiently *explicit*.

Q. In what fituation was Mr. Frost at that time ?

A. He was Solicitor and Agent of Lord Hood.

Q. You told us before, that *you* was a *friend* to Lord Hood. I fuppofe you only *know* him as a Candidate for Weftminfter ?

[Here the Witnefs fwelled into confequence.]

A. Sir, *I have the* HONOUR *to know* Lord Hood *perfonally !*

Q. Did you *never* tell Mr. Smith that Mr. Rose *would pay him?*

A. I never did.

Q. How then was Smith to be paid?

A. He was to be paid like the reft, by Mr. Frost and Mr. Jackson.

Q. From what fund ?

A. That I do not know.

Q. Was Mr. Smith never introduced to Mr. Rose ?

[Here again the Gentleman affumed an air of dignity.]

A. Sir, I *had the honour of* PRODUCING

the

the INTERVIEW *between* THESE TWO GEN-
TLEMEN !

CROSS-EXAMINED by Mr. BEARCROFT.

Q. Now attend, *Clubb.* Has not Lord
Hood's Committee paid Mr. SMITH a great
deal of money?

A. They undoubtedly have.

Q. You faid that you have mentioned
the name of SMITH to Mr. ROSE ?

A. I put down the *names* of Mr. *Smith*'s
houfe and of his *Brother's* houfe ; and *fuggefted* to Mr. ROSE and Mr. STEEL, that
they were proper houfes.

Q. Was any other perfon prefent ?

[Here a good deal of hefitation and unwillingnefs en-
fued.]

A. I CANNOT RECOLLECT who was in
the room when that was mentioned.

Q. (Mr. ERSKINE) You *muft* recollect,
Sir."

[At laft out came the anfwer]

A. Mr. PITT *was in the Room !*

Q. You fay, then, that Mr. PITT was in

the

the room with Mr. Rose and Mr. Steel, at the time *you fuggefted to them the propriety* of opening Mr. Smith's houfe for Lord Hood and *his Friends?*

A. He was.

Q. What made you think that Mr. Smith's houfe was a houfe more proper to be opened than any other?

A. Becaufe he was a PATRIOTIC MAN, *and I thought he would go ANY LENGTHS in the Caufe; and therefore I recommended him to* Mr. PITT, Mr. STEEL, *and* Mr. ROSE.

Q. You fay he was a *patriotic* man—Why do you fay fo?

A. Becaufe he had gone 20 or 30l. out of pocket, and therefore *I recommended* him to thefe Gentlemen: I believed him to be ftaunch in the Caufe ; he detected a great number of bad votes polled for Lord John Townshend.

Q. I believe, *at laft, he began to flacken?*

A. No, *he did not flacken,* but *perfevered,* and went A GREAT LENGTH indeed ; but

it

it was *never* fuppofed that he would *charge* any thing for his TROUBLE !

Q. Did Mr. ROSE employ him ?

A. No, he was *employed* by MYSELF *! I recommended* him to Mr. ROSE ; and he *having complained* he could get nothing for his TROUBLE and EXPENCE, I applied to a " certain Gentleman."

[Lord KENYON, from his impartial love of Juftice, here interpofed his authority, and took up the examination of the Witnefs himfelf]

Q. Who was that " *certain Gentleman,*" Sir ?

A. I *beg* you will hear me—I *fpoke* and *recommended* him to a " *certain Gentleman.*"

Q. (Lord KENYON)—*Who? Who?*

A. I beg you will excufe me.

Q. Lord (KENYON)—No, Sir, *you must answer the question.*

A. I SPOKE TO Mr. ROSE.

[Here the bufinefs was interrupted by a burft of laughter.]

Q. (Mr. BEARCROFT,) *What* did *you* fay to Mr. ROSE ?

A. I told

A. I told him this man *had* GONE a confiderable way in detecting bad votes polled for Lord JOHN TOWNSHEND, and that he could detect five or fix hundred of them, but could *not* PROCEED *without money.*

Q. Well, *what anfwer* did Mr. ROSE make to that?

A. He faid, " Mr. Smith might give them *victuals and drink,* but he muft not go too far. He goes too great lengths; he muft not go too far." I told Mr. ROSE that he was *very ftrenuous in the Caufe.*

RE-EXAMINED *by Mr. MINGAY.*

Q. You fay then, CLUBB, that when you mentioned the bufinefs to Mr. ROSE he had no objections to allow SMITH for the *victuals and drink,* but defired that he would not go on too far?

A. He did.

Q. I think you faid that Mr. Smith had done fome bufinefs, and had put himfelf to fome expence in detecting thefe bad votes before you mentioned him to Mr. Rofe?

A. He had. Mr. Rofe faid he was a troublefome

troublefome fellow; and he frequently *extorted* an *anfwer* from Mr. RosE.

Q. Well, Sir, when you came back from Mr. RosE, did you *communicate this converfation* which paffed between you and Mr. RosE, to Mr. Smith?

A. When I came back, I told Mr. Smith he might *go on* to collect bad votes, but muft not go on too far.

Mr. Frost the Solicitor was then called and fworn; but before he gave his teftimony, he addreffed the Bench as follows:

" *My Lord,*
" I am fworn: but before I proceed to
" give my teftimony on my oath, con-
" fidering the fituation in which I ftand
" to the Parties in this Caufe, I wifh to
" have fome directions from your Lord-
" fhip, whether I fhould anfwer fome
" queftions that may be put to me by the
" Counfel. I prefcribed this rule to
" myfelf "—

E   Lord

Lord Kenyon.——" Don't make a
fpeech, Sir. Tell me what you wifh me
to do—the Law admits of no fuch de-
licacy."

Mr. Frost then proceeded in his evidence as follows :

" *My Lord, and Gentlemen of the Jury,*

" The contefted Election for Weftmin-
" fter ended on the fourth of Auguft,
" 1788. In the months of September and
" October following Mr. Smith came
" frequently to me, and brought me lifts
" of bad votes, which he had difcovered
" at the preceding Election. After fre-
" quent vifits, and fome circumftances
" having paffed between Mr. Smith and
" me, I thought it neceffary to go to Mr.
" Rose, to afk him if Smith was a pro-
" per perfon to be trufted, becaufe the com-
" munications were of fome confequence.
" When I had an interview with Mr.
" Rose, I told him of the vifits which
" I had from Smith, refpecting thefe bad
" votes, and afked him whether Smith
                " might

" might be trufted ? Mr. ROSE SAID,
" I MIGHT WITH GREAT SAFETY TRUST
" SMITH, FOR THEY KNEW HIM WELL."
" This was in the Treafury. Cn the
" 28th of October, I had a lift of bad
" votes from Mr. SMITH, which I exa-
" mined during a long period, when Mr.
" SMITH and I underftood each other.
" It was by Mr. ROSE's direction, that Mr.
" SMITH had collected bad votes in Sep-
" tember and October. He returned me
" lifts of upwards of fix hundred bad votes.
" This bufinefs he performed, in my opi-
" nion, with abilities and zeal, and his
" bill was extremely reafonable. After he
" had gone fome length, he applied to me
" repeatedly for money. I kept a diftinct
" account of thofe perfons employed by
" the *Treafury* from thofe whom I em-
" ployed, as *Agent of Lord* HOOD. Upon
" my refufing to give him money, he
" brought me this bill."—

[Here Mr. FROST produced a bill, delivered to him
by the Plaintiff: It amounted to 59l. In this bill Mr.
ROSE was intitled debtor to the Plaintiff; on which
appeared, in the hand-writing of Mr. ROSE,—"MODE-
" RATE, AND OUGHT TO BE PAID."]

FROST

Frost then continued his narrative.—
" After I had feen Mr. Rose, 1 told Mr.
" Smith, that if he would bring a letter
" to me from Mr. Rose, 1 would pay him
" for his fervices in this bufinefs."

Mr. Frost was here afked by Mr. Mingay, whether Mr. Rose had not told
him, that he meant to do Smith fome
favour? To which Mr. Frost replied,
that he did not recollect.—But on Mr.
Mingay mentioning the Excise, and
Lord Kenyon requefting that the *whole
truth* might come out, Mr. Frost an-
fwered in thefe words :

" *When I was fpeaking to Mr.* Rose, *of*
" Smith, *Mr. Rose faid, that there was*
" *fomething of a* Prosecution *going on*
" *with the* EXCISE *againft* Smith, *and as*
" *a mark of the* Trust *and* Confidence
" *they had in* him, *they had* INTER-
" FERED, *and* STEPT IN *to* SERVE
" HIM ; *but in what way was not ex-*
" *plained.*

" The

" The Lifts were brought to me com-
" pleat in a long Roll, which had been
" delivered to Mr. Rose; and he never
" denied that he was to pay Mr. Smith.
" The Plaintiff has no claim upon me or
" my Lord Hood."

Mr. Erskine.—" My Lord this is our
Cafe."

DEFENCE.

Mr. Bearcroft, on behalf of the Honourable Secretary, made the following
fpeech:

" *May it pleafe your Lordfhip, and you Gentlemen
of the Jury.*

" My learned friend, Mr. Erfkine, has
got on very triumphantly hitherto in this
Caufe; and it is extremely entertain-
ing to go with the wind, whenever
there is an attack made on perfons in
the fituation of the prefent Defendant.
How *wife* it is to refift this demand, I
fhall not fay; but if there is any thing
unwife

unwife in it, *I am not the caufe.* Gentlemen, you have not yet heard the whole
of this Caufe: when you have, in God's
name, do Juftice ; but ftop, and do not
proceed on fuch fuggeftions as have been
made to you in the opening of this Cafe.
My learned friend told you, " That a great
" number of obfervations in this Caufe
" might prefent themfelves to a mind dif-
" pofed to mifchief; but that he fhould
" ftudioufly avoid all fuch obferva-
" tions."

" He fpent nine tenths of the whole time
he took up in his opening, in fuggefting,
" That the expence was defrayed out of
" the *public purfe*;" but, Gentlemen, has
this been proved ? It has not. If it was
fo, *it was very difhonourable :* but no man
is to prefume it, without proof; and I do
not believe there is a tittle of truth in it.
It has been proved that the Plaintiff's
name was mentioned to Mr. ROSE at different times. Mr. ROSE, at different
times, if you pleafe, *encouraged* him. The
Secretary of the Treafury was the Friend
of

of Lord Hood, and had occafionally given his opinion.—

Lord Kenyon. " Mr. Bearcroft, what do you fay to one piece of Evidence, to wit, as to the Bill?"—' To Gorge Rose, Debtor;' " and the De-" fendant, fo far from denying it, having marked on it," ' moderate, and ought to be ' paid.'

Mr. Bearcroft. "My Lord, Mr. Rose did not interfere further, than became any Gentleman who was a Friend to Lord Hood. I know I ftand in an *awkward fitu-ation*; but I fhall ftate an anfwer; and I know *I muſt ſtate a ſtrong anſwer* to this piece of Evidence. This Election, then, as we all know, was carried on by a Committee: on the part of Lord Hood, there is a bill that was delivered in by the prefent Plaintiff to that Committee: it contained a great number of the items of the bill delivered to Mr. Rose by Mr. Froft, and which is paid.—I fhall be ready to affent to any propofal that may be thought proper in this cafe.

'Lord

Lord KENYON. " Mr. Bearcroft, you cannot without *exceeding strong evidence indeed*, get over the Bill delivered.—Here is a Bill, in which GEO. ROSE, Efquire, is made Debtor ; and it is not denied that he is anfwerable for the payment of it."

Mr. BEARCROFT.—" My Lord, I hope and truft that I fhall be heard to the end of my Defence for my Client; and that you, Gentlemen of the Jury, will do him juftice, although he is a *Secretary to the Treafury*. All that I defire, is, that I may have an opportunity of ftating the Cafe clearly. Mr. Froft has told you, that a Bill was delivered, in which GEORGE ROSE was made Debtor, and that he allowed it to be moderate, and that it ought to be paid. The prefent Plaintiff, however, is calling on Mr. ROSE for this Bill, amongft the reft, for certain bufinefs fuppofed to be done on the credit of Mr. ROSE, when, in fact, Smith did not give credit to Mr. ROSE for the prefent Bill, but to Lord HOOD's Committee."

Mr.

Mr. Erſkine.—" No! No! all is for buſineſs done and money paid for Mr. Roſe to other people ; excluſive of buſineſs ſettled by the Agents of Lord Hood's, Committee."—

Mr. Bearcroft *(holding a Bill in his hand)* ſaid, " Gentlemen of the Jury, This Bill is compoſed of articles for eating and drinking, and money paid. There is an *item* for finding out bad votes, Bludgeon-Men, &c. oppoſite to which there is a blank. It concludes with the words " humbly ſubmitted." Now, Gentlemen, the amount of this Bill, excluſive of this article, for which nothing is charged, is 129l. 6s. 9d. I ſhall prove that he received this ſum from the hands of Mr. Jackſon, and for which the Plaintiff gave him a Receipt in full of all demands. But it is ſaid—" here are other demands, for articles of a different kind." In the Bill itſelf he makes a charge for collecting upwards of ſix hundred bad votes. But *whom* does he charge with the payment of this ſum?

F   The

The perfon, to be fure, to whom he delivers this Bill. But if he goes away with 129l. and gives a Receipt in full of all demands, with this article in the Bill, I truft that my Lord and you will be of opinion, that the Plaintiff thought, at this time, that he had no further demand upon any body."

Mr. BALDWIN requefted his Lordfhip to obferve the diftinction between the two Bills.

Lord KENYON. " Mr. Baldwin, if you will give me leave, I think I have juft fenfe enough to comprehend this Bill."

Mr. *Jackfon* was called, on the part of the Defendant, to prove the fubftance of the Defence, and that the Plaintiff had no Caufe of Action. He gave the following Narrative, on Oath:

" As Mr. Froft had refufed to pay a
" number of Bills on account of Lord
" Hood,

" Hood, I was defired, by his Lordfhip,
" fome time about February, 1790, to
" collect in all the outftanding Bills. I
" accordingly fent to all the Chairmen of
" the feveral Committees, and had Bills
" fent in to a very confiderable amount.
" Mr. Smith called on me, and delivered
" to me the Bill which I have now in my
" hand. I afked Mr. Smith for the Bill
" of 59l. which makes the firft item in
" *this* Bill. Mr. Smith faid, he had deli-
" vered it in to Mr. Rofe, and he believed
" Mr. Rofe had delivered it to Mr. Froft,
" and that he could not get it from Mr.
" Froft, becaufe they were not upon good
" terms.--129l. 6s. 9d. was the whole of his
" Bill, exclufive of this article, viz. *fix*
" *hundred bad votes, bludgeon-men, &c.* ' hum -
" *bly fubmitted.*' I told him, Mr. Smith,
" there are charges here that are very li-
" beral ; but, if I pay you 129l. 6s. 6d.
" I fuppofe you will be fatisfied. He he-
" fitated a little, and then faid, ' he fhould.'
" I would not have paid him one fhilling,
" except on condition of his having ac-

F 2   " cepted

".cepted of this 129l. 6s. 6d. in full of
" all demands I told him repeatedly,
" that I had nothing to do with Mr. Rofe,
" and that I was only to examine the Bills
" of Lord Hood, to fee if they contained
" the whole of the refpective demands. I
" alfo told the Plaintiff, that he muft fettle
" every thing."

On his Crofs-Examination he repeated
this evidence, adding, " I know nothing
" of Mr. Rofe; I was only Lord Hood's
" Agent, and had no direction to pay for
" thefe bad votes."

The Right Honourable *Thomas Steel*,
Paymafter of the King's Forces, attend-
ing, in obedience to a Subpœna, to give
his evidence on this Trial, faid, the ur-
gency of public bufinefs demanded his
attendance at another place: he begged
permiffion therefore to retire, to which
Mr. Erfkine politely and obligingly con-
fented.

REPLY.

REPLY.

Mr. Erſkine, on the part of the Plaintiff, made the following Reply.

*May it pleaſe your Lordſhip, and you Gentle-
men of the Jury,*

I am perſuaded that my learned Friend,
Bearcroft, after he goes home, on a few
moments refledtion, will eaſily perceive
the *prudence* of one part of his Addreſs to
you.---I had my reaſons for being diſpoſed
to treat Mr. Roſe with great courteſy and
reſpedt. I have ſome *private reaſons,*
which it is unneceſſary to ſtate, and *I con-
ſulted with my friends how far I could do it
conſiſtently with my ſituation here—how far
I could do compleat juſtice to my Client, and
preſerve that courteſy and reſpedt which every Gentleman would wiſh to ſhew to another.*
I did draw a veil over this buſineſs. I
was *unwilling* to impute any thing crimi-
nal to Mr. Roſe, any thing improper, any
thing

thing *indelicate*, any thing *inconfiſtent* with the *duties* of his *Situatian*, any thing *diſ-honourable* to the Character of a *Secretary of the Treaſury*. I opened the Caſe, by ſtat-ing, that he might have done it as *a pri-vate friend of* Lord Hood, or for the pur-poſe of ſupporting the *principle of a Bill to be brought before Parliament*, and not as the *Agent* of *Corruption*; for *ſuch conduct*, from *ſuch motives*, muſt neceſſarily excite your *reſentment*, as well as the *indignation* of the *Public*. Nothing ſhall provoke me to deviate from the line of moderation which I originally ſet out with; and there-fore, ſince it is not at all neceſſary for the ends of juſtice, I repeat the obſervations I formerly made, namely, that I *am much more willing* to ſuppoſe that Mr. Roſe has *nothing* to anſwer for, than that he *has*.

" He has certainly attended with very lit-tle diſcretion to a trifling demand, which is as clearly made out, as the price of a halfpenny Roll which is ſold in a market. *I wiſh* to conſider George Roſe, Eſq. at pre-ſent,

fent, merely as a man ftanding in a Court
of Juftice. *I wifh to forget* that he is a
Member of Parliament; *I wifh to forget*
that he is a *Secretary* of the *Treafury*; that
he is a friend of Lord Hood, and that Lord
Hood and Lord John Townfhend were
Candidates at that Election. It is needlefs
for me to ftate how *neceffary* it is to the
People, and the *falvation* of the *State*, that
the *Reprefentative Body* fhould be *freely-
elected*; and that the Reprefentatives *fo elected*,
ought to carry on the Legiflative part of
the Conftitution. I hope *few* Caufes like
this will ever make their *appearance* in a *Court
of Juftice*. In the firft place, one cannot
help lamenting, that, for the paltry fum
of 110l. the amount of an *Election* Bill,
a *Man in a public ftation*, and *one* of the Secretaries of the *Treafury*, fhould *permit* a
demand *fo juftly* due, to be *publicly difcuffed
in a Court of Juftice*; and that we fhould
be *obliged* to examine *this* Election Bill by
the *unwilling teftimony* of this Mr. Clubb,
a Meffenger of the Treafury. If *he had gone*

on

*on a little further, I should have applied to
my Lord to commit him!*

[Here Mr. Erskine recited the principal parts of
Mr. Clubb's evidence.]

He is, said he, a *profligate* and *corrupt
Witness*, coming into a Court of Justice to
speak *against* what *he knows*, but *he at last
proved* the *Plaintiff's case.* We next call
Mr. *Frost*, and then let us see what sort
of a case this is. The Plaintiff makes out a
bill, and calls on Mr. *Frost*, who says he has
nothing at all to do with the business. The
bill is next presented to *George Rose*, Esq.
which he examines, and afterwards writes
on it, " That it was moderate, and ought
to be paid." Would ever Mr. *Rose* have
done this, if he had thought that Mr.
Smith was never to have been paid ? It is
I who want to *protect* Mr. *Rose*. My learned friend wants to *degrade* him to the
level of a common Attorney for Lord
Hood—I want to *exalt* him. Mr. *Frost*
then tells you, that this man conducted
himself

himfelf with a great deal of zeal and abilities; that he had actually detected fix
hundred bad votes; and the demand, Mr.
Froſt thought, was extremely reafonable.
When the bill comes in, it is a hard
thing, it feems, for Mr. *Roſe* to pay it.
" *Take it out of honeſt Mr. John Bull's*
" *pocket !* There is no great harm in tak-
" ing a *ſlice* out of the *Exciſe,* or *public*
" *Revenue,* to *defray a little of the Expence*
" *of the Election of a Miniſterial Member*
" *of Parliament."* Gentlemen, there is
nothing plainer, than that if I can *ſave* a
man from a *hundred pounds penalty,* it is
the *ſame* as *paying him* an *hundred pounds;*
and if *this hundred pounds penalty* would
otherwiſe have gone into the *Treaſury,* it is
ſelf-evident, that *this hundred* was *in effect*
" *paid out of the Treaſury."*

I at laſt come to the Defence, and a
more mean, paltry, ſhabby, contemptible
one, I never ſaw brought into a Court of
Juſtice. Here is a man, who ſtood in a
double capacity, for having done buſineſs

G for

for Mr. *Rose*, on *his own retainer*, and *also*
for Lord *Hood*.

Says Mr. *Jackson*, I never knew Mr.
Rose. What bufinefs then had Mr. *Jackfon* with Mr. *Rose's debt?* And yet Mr.
Jackfon is pleafed to fay to Mr. *Smith*—
Although I know nothing of Mr. *Rose*,
and although I am *only* Agent to Lord
Hood, yet I will *not* pay you for the bufinefs that was done for Lord *Hood*, unlefs you give me a *difcharge in full of all
demands for the bufinefs alfo that has been
done for Mr Rose!*

Gentlemen of the Jury, independent of
the *law* of this cafe, I proteft to you I cannot difcover (I confefs to you I am a dull
man) **the** common decency, the common
honefty, or the propriety of any part of
this tranfaction. The Plaintiff, Mr. *Smith*,
has been at great labour. It is confefled
on all hands, that he has difcovered upwards of fix hundred bad votes, polled
for Lord *John Townfhend*, which, by
                                        the

the induftry of my Client, paffed for nothing.

Gentlemen, I put this queftion to you :
—When a man has a fair demand on A,
and A fays to him, unlefs you will give
up your demand on B, I will not difcharge you ; what muft you think of A ?
*I will fhew my regard to the Public, by not
preffing this matter any further.* Gentlemen in the *fituation* of the *Defendant, will
do well to beware how they defend fuch ac-
tions !*

Lord *Kenyon's* Addrefs to the Jury.

Gentlemen of the Jury,
We have nothing to do with the *prudence*
or *good fenfe* that has brought this Caufe
into public difcuffion. Since it is brought
here, we are to do juftice, as well as we
can, between the Parties. We muft con-
fider it as a demand made by one individual on another individual, on a con-
tract either expreffed or implied. And it
G 2   does

does appear to me, that nobody was more anfwerable for this demand than Mr. *Rofe*. If the Witnefies for the Plaintiff were to be believed, Mr. *Rofe* directed the Plaintiff to go on to find out bad votes. It muft be fuppofed that Mr. *Smith* was to be paid by fomebody, and no other perfon being acceffary to this bufinefs, I proteft I do not know to whom to afcribe the order, but to Mr. *Rofe*. Mr. *Smith* had frequent converfations upon this fubject with him, and upon the whole of the evidence, Mr. *Rofe* muft be confidered as debtor to the Plaintiff.

But here another queftion arifes, and that is " Whether this demand has been " paid?" This, Gentlemen, perhaps is not ultimately a very important Action.

Mr. *Jackfon* has told you, that Mr. *Smith's* bill with him amounted to 129l. 6s. 6d. and there was another article, to wit, for collecting fix hundred bad votes, for which nothing was charged; but thefe words were

were added, "humbly fubmitted." Mr.
Jackfon told him, that he would fettle
every thing, and that he afked him, Whether 129l. would not fatisfy his *whole* demand? The Plaintiff hefitated for fome
time, which he could not do about the
Amount of the Bill, for *that* was only
129l. and therefore it muft have been
about the Article of the Bad Votes, for
which nothing was charged, but only
" humbly fubmitted." *If* that evidence
is *true*, undoubtedly it fhews, that he
was paid the *whole* of the demand. The
whole of the demand ftated in the Bill,
amounted exactly to the fum which Mr.
Jackfon offered to pay.

I look at this Caufe as other people do.
Upon the whole of the Evidence, if you
are of opinion that the payment of this
Bill by Mr. Jackfon meant to go in fatis-
faction of the *whole demand*, your Verdict
will be for the *Defendant*; but on the
contrary, if you are of a different opinion,
and think that this demand is for *other*
fervices

fervices *not included* in the Bill paid by Jackfon, you will find a Verdict for the *Plaintiff*.

Gentlemen of the Jury, it is your peculiar province to decide in this cafe. The Conftitution of the Country has placed it in your hands, and I have no doubt but you will do fubftantial juftice between the Parties.

The JURY immediately found a

VERDICT *for the* PLAINTIFF:

Damages---One Hundred & Ten Pounds, Five Shillings,

BEING THE

WHOLE AMOUNT OF HIS DEMAND.

RE-

REFLECTIONS,

ADDRESSED TO

GEORGE ROSE, Esq.

⸻⸻

YOUR King's Bench Defeat will open
the eyes of a deluded people. They will
infer from that decifion, Sir, *why* their
taxes are multiplied, and *how* an *incorrupt*
Adminiftration procure their Majorities.
It is now upon record in a Court of Juftice, that a Treafury Secretary, in the
prefence of his immaculate mafter, fo far
degrades the character of a Statefman, as
to hire men for the defpicable purpofe of
Election intrigue. If, Sir, there can be
any act more unbecoming than this, it is
in not paying the man you employed.

Your *friend* Clubb, although he meant
to bring you off, was fo bungling an
evidence, that he was the chief means of
cafting you. In one part he fwore, that
he never told Smith that *you* were to pay
him.

him. In another part he fwore, that *you* told him to inform Smith to give his *men* victuals and drink, but *not to go too far*. Do not you, Sir, perceive an unlucky inconfiftency in thefe two parts? As to not going too far, furely you could not mean it in detecting bad votes; for, had it been poffible he could have fet afide all Lord John Townfhend's, it would have been only what you wanted? It could not mean victuals and drink to Smith's men, as thofe articles had been already ordered by you? Then, Sir, what did you mean by not going too far? The only way in which I can explain it, is from what appears, that your friend Clubb faid, in the prefence of his Majefty's Minifter, the prefent Paymafter of the Forces, and yourfelf, when recommending Smith to them, " That he was a ftaunch *patriot*, " and would go *any lengths*." Knowing his bold capability, from this good character, your prudence fuggefted, I fuppofe, that he muft not go too far, as it might lead you into a fcrape. Do not

you

you think, Sir, that the ftaunch *Pat-Riots*, at Birmingham, have gone too far? I am fure you, and every good man, is of that opinion. May fome of their ringleaders remain *unpaid*, and their fecret abettors will be dragged forward into a Court of Juftice, as you lately have been!

Your *friend* Clubb is certainly a man of very great confequence. Although but a Treafury Runner, he *fuggefts opinions*, and *directs*, indeed, the very Chiefs of Adminiftration! This mighty Meffenger! this winged Treafury God, *Mercury*, even advifes and controuls our immaculate State *Jupiter* himfelf! For is it not now proved in a Court of Juftice, that he fuggefted! that he advifed the Minifter's Secretaries, in his very prefence!

Of what wonderful and weighty confequence then is a Treafury Meffenger! Thefe Meffengers, inftead of fitting in your Lobby, where you yourfelf have often fat formerly, fhould fit in Parliament, and enjoy the moft ample falaries! Why

H fhould

fhould fuch a Treafury Meffenger as Clubb
fuggeft, advife, and direct the *Minister*,
and his *Secretaries*, and have no more fa-
lary for a *whole Year's fervice*, than you,
Sir, have for *every fingle Day in the Year*?
At the Tax-Office, had you not but Fifty
Pounds a Year? Now, it is reported, that
you have Fifty Pounds a Day! George
Rofe, the Secretary, has a greater income
than the Republican Emperor of the Ame-
rican States, the illuftrious Wafhington!

Your friend Clubb, in all the haughty
exterior of your mafter, Pitt, it appears,
" informs the Court that he had the ho-
" nour of producing the firft interview
" between Mr. Smith, the Publican, and
" Mr. Rofe, the Secretary!"

In another place, your friend Clubb tells
the Court, with much pomp, " *I* recom-
" mended Mr. Smith to Mr. Pitt, Mr.
" Steel, and Mr. Rofe!"

Again, your friend Clubb boafts in
Court, " that the Commander in Chief
" of

" of the Britifh Fleet, Lord Hood, is his
" *perfonal friend !*"

Your friend Clubb, like Middleton,
could *not* recollect, at one time, who was
in the room, when he mentioned to you
and Mr. Steel, " that Mr. Smith was a
" proper perfon to ferve them, as he was
" a ftaunch *patriot,* and *would go any*
" *lengths !*"

But your friend Clubb, in another part
of his evidence, recollects that

" *HIS MAJESTY's FIRST LORD OF THE*
  TREASURY! and
" *BRITAIN's HEAVEN-BORN MINISTER!*

" was in the room with you and friend
" Clubb, when you fettled the bargain for
" employing Smith !"

Your friend Clubb fays, that Smith frequently extorts an anfwer from you. An
old Officer in the Army, who was prefent
at the Trial, remarked upon this, " That
" if we were to examine all thofe Gentle-

" men

" men in the Treafury anti-chamber, who,
" while peevifhly waiting upon you, in
" deep chagrin at eternal procraftination
" and perpetual difappointment, examin-
" ing the large Map of London hanging
" there, nineteen out of twenty would
" fubfcribe to the truth of your friend
" Clubb's doctrine."

Lord Hawkefbury knows that Map well. So do you. Both of you, I am told, have been ftudents there, for obtaining a complete knowledge of political geography, among the Meffengers; although, no doubt, you ftudied at very different periods.

If the prefent Adminiftation, Sir, fhould unaccountably continue much longer in office, I really think that your friend Clubb fhould fometimes prefide in · the Treafury Board Room, as he has often done *below stairs*, at the *Board of Election*; and he ought certainly to be ennobled, for his fuperior knowledge, his great zeal, and his inceffant activity. Indeed, Sir, many, not
half

half fo deferving as Clubb, have been ennobled by your Collea; ues. In fuch a
cafe, I would advife you to perfuade your
friend to adopt his title from his name, as
it is fo very fignificant. It would moft
pointedly indicate his deep erudition a-
mong the *Bludgeoneers*, in all future Elections whatever.

But enough of Clubb; as, if I may be
allowed to pun, you are by this time,
Sir, more difgufted with that Clubb than
the French King is with the *Club* of *Ja-*
cobins, or *others* with the philanthropic
Club of that *amiable*, *learned*, and *benevo-*
lent martyr, PRIESTLY! Having mentioned Prieftly, I much wonder, had *Price*
been alive on the *fourteenth*, if the *populace*,
(i. e. in my dictionary, the *mob)* would
have paid an *igneal* vifit to his unhallow-
ed Meeting-houfe? I rather think it
would have been in their lift; and I,
therefore, fo far rejoice in the Doctor's
death, as that circumftance has very pro-
bably faved the peace of the capital.

I can-

I cannot help here congratulating the *inoſtenſible* Lord Hawkeſbury, in the abſence of Mr. Dundas, who, as Treaſurer of the Navy, was reviewing the fleet at Portſmouth ; ſo far interfering himſelf in the Secretary's affairs, as to write to the unfortunate ſufferers at Birmingham, with proffers to ſend the moſt eminent Counſel to aſſiſt in their enquiries concerning the origin of the Riots, under the direction of the Attorney and Solicitor General. With all my predilection for the mild Mr. Macdonald, and the ſhrewd Sir John Scott, the King's Attorney and Solicitor General, I beg, Sir, you will recommend theſe Gentlemen to call in, as eminent Counſel, the Prince of Wales's Attorney and Solicitor General, Meſſrs. *Erſkine* and *Pigott*. I ſhall, in that caſe, have very great hopes of the *grand authors* of this horrid plot being diſcovered ; and ſurely to obtain ſuch a diſcovery, neither expence, time, nor talents, ought to be ſpared. Would it not likewiſe be worth while to enquire, why the ſoldiers were ſo long in reaching Birmingham, and how

the

the *furious populace* were *so well trained*, and so *humane all of a sudden*, as to *train off*, without *one* life being loft, at the approach of the military?

Had the *Diffenters* raifed fuch a mob, I wonder if the military would have been fo tardy in their march, and the lives of the *vile mob* (not the populace then!) fo miraculoufly have been fpared? I fee, by the papers, that the *police populace* in Dublin, too, have been firing, on that evening, *a few rounds of powder and ball* in the ftreets, upon harmlefs paffengers, by way of a *feu de joie*, which, very luckily, was ended, without rifing to a *Birmingham illumination*. Is it not ftrange, nay unaccountable, how the *populace* of Birmingham and Dublin fhould, on that day, agree in endeavouring to deftroy the *friends of freedom*, and the *Britifh Conftitution?* The train was well laid; but I am fure you rejoice with me in this, Sir, that all thofe Riots have ceafed.

To return: enough being faid of your
fiiend

friend Club—What a ferious charge does .
Mr. Froft make againft you, Sir, refpect-
. ing the *Excife-fine* of Smith ? Mr. Froft
is a refpectable character ; and your anti-
pathy to Lord Lanfdowne, the noble-
man who firft drew you forth from
obfcurity, ought not fo far to have ex-
tended, as to profcribe Mr. Froft, becaufe he, like you, has been patronifed
by him. You will, I fear, foon rue the
day when you quarrelled with Lord
Hood's Agent. He has both fpirit, per-
feverance, and *anecdote*, to undo you
totally in the public opinion. The *Excife-fine alone*, if properly handled, of
which there can be no doubt, will com-
pletely do your bufinefs : and after being
punifhed by public cenfure, you will, perhaps, be permitted to retire to Cuffnels ;
and efcape, by feclufion, the fcornful,
pointed finger of your indignant Country.

ALFRED.